KALAALLIT NUNAAT
LAND OF THE PEOPLE

To Rich,

Best polar wishes!

[signature]

Tricorn Books

KALAALLIT NUNAAT - LAND OF THE PEOPLE

Photography and design © Alex Hibbert

ISBN 978-0-9571074-4-1

A CIP catalogue record for this book is available
from the British Library.

Published 2012 by Tricorn Books,
a trading name of 131 Design Ltd.
131 High Street, Old Portsmouth, PO1 2HW

www.alexhibbert.com
www.tricornbooks.co.uk

Printed and bound in Great Britain

KALAALLIT NUNAAT
LAND OF THE PEOPLE

A PHOTOGRAPHIC ACCOUNT OF GREENLAND

Greenland is a land of contrasts. Its interior is dominated by the second largest ice sheet on Earth whilst the periphery supports a thriving population, the Kalaallit (or Greenlandic Inuit). As a true frontier nation, the combination of one of the most brutal and hostile wildernesses and some of the most welcoming traditional communities makes Greenland one of the world's special places.

Since 2500 BC there have been successive cultures living in various areas of Greenland. These were mostly in the southern and western regions, where the long fjords and rolling hills provided a glimpse of an opportunity to sustain a lasting existence in a barren sub-arctic and arctic environment. Today, after dozens of migrations and settlements by various groups, communities exist on the western, eastern and southern coasts. The north coast, bordering the vast Arctic Ocean, has been extensively travelled by the Inuit but only a handful of tiny villages survive on the north-west coast. The most northerly, Siorapaluk, supports fewer than seventy people and others fewer than twenty-five.

The southern half of Greenland has a halo of larger settlements around its coast, including Kangerlussuaq, Illulissat, Tasiilaq, Kulusuk and the capital, Nuuk. Some areas now support populations in the low thousands with modest but effective developments including schools and hospitals. With low levels of employment, a highly restrictive landscape and an unavoidable remoteness, traditional pursuits such as hunting, fishing and driving dog teams still play a vital role.

In winter, the island is plunged into a permanent twilight or darkness, depending on the extremity of the latitude. Life still goes on despite the regular storms and low temperatures, with children going to school and villagers travelling out onto the frozen sea in the search for fauna. As the sun returns in the spring, the snowy blanket still smothers the hills, mountains and waterways of the coast but slowly melts away as the days become longer and temperatures rise. The summer provides an opportunity for the locals to travel with ease using boats and kayaks, whilst the mountains are briefly uncovered before the winter returns to complete the relentless cycle.

My own travels around the communities of Greenland and the mammoth icecap which dominates it began whilst barely out of my teenage years. My main interest has always been for the sterile brutality of the icecap and the human challenge that presents. It is impossible, however, to seek the extremes that the white wilderness has to offer without becoming entranced by the people and landscapes through which you must first pass. The warmth, generosity and sheer resilience of the people who call Greenland home is perhaps without equal. Their Greenlandic sledge dogs, found nowhere else in the world, are indispensable companions and workers. They unsurprisingly play a major part in any photographic essay.

This book has been designed to achieve two ends. Firstly, to give the imagery total dominance and room to breathe without the distraction of text overload. Secondly, to give equal attention to the many facets of a vulnerable part of our world which is both magical and at times, terrifying.

THE PEOPLE

Tasiilaq village in spring

Amidst one of the low-pressure weather systems which persistently plague the coast in the spring months, a brief break in the clouds unveils the mountainous surroundings of the largest settlement in East Greenland.

Canon G10; 1/2000 sec at f4; ISO 80.

Contrasts of the summer

In a similar view to the previous
photograph but five months later, the
landscape has transformed. Little ice
remains, due to the near-permanent
sunlight, and the rocky coastline is
exposed.

Canon 5D Mark II + 17-40mmL; 1/350
sec at f8; ISO 100.

Taxi of the Arctic

By far the quickest and most efficient way to travel across sea ice and the lowlands is by dog sled. Fuel for snowmobiles is expensive and a helicopter charter over-the-top for most. The dogs just require occasional feeding and a little attention in return for an aesthetic journey.

Canon 5D Mark II + 17-40mmL; 1/125 sec at f9.5; ISO 100.

Hunters with dog team

Local hunters need to regularly move along the edge of the sea ice in order to maximise the chance of a kill. The dogs have a habit of getting their rope 'traces' tangled and so need to be reorganised before moving the sledge to another more hopeful spot for seal hunting.

Canon 5D Mark II + 17-40mmL; 1/125 sec at f5.6; ISO 100.

Fish drying on racks

The fjords surrounding the settlements
of Eastern Greenland are rich with life,
including many species of fish. Villagers
supplement their diets with large
quantities of local catches. They are salted
and dried on racks before eating.

Canon 5D Mark II + 24-85mm; 1/60 sec
at f8; ISO 200.

Tradition meets modern culture

A child's drum kit sits outside a traditional house in Tasiilaq village. Despite the strong emphasis on traditional skills and culture in Greenland, modern music, cinema and entertainment has well and truly arrived.

Canon 1D Mark II N + 19-35mm; 1/30 sec at f5; ISO 800.

Blue skies follow heavy snowfall

Late winter and early spring tend to bring
the most unreliable and snowy conditions
to the communities. The colourful wood
and concrete buildings are designed with
this in mind. The majority, however, still
lack running water and waste disposal
plumbing.

Canon G10; 1/2000 sec at f4.5; ISO 80.

Man-made open water on seal hunt

The resulting 'seal-trap' left after hunter
Georg Utuaq used his kayak to break up
the thin, recently frozen ice, twenty miles
from Kulusuk. The open water that is left
can provide a breathing hole for seals and
helps the hunters attract their quarry.

Canon 5D Mark II + 17-40mmL; 1/125
sec at f8; ISO 100.

Home to three hundred

These small houses on the outskirts of
Kulusuk represent the equivalent of a
suburb in a European city - even more
isolated and cheaper than those nearer
to the shop and natural harbour. Ever
since the Greenlandic Inuit began to live
in buildings made from imported timber,
they have painted them in bright colours.

Canon 5D Mark II + 17-40mmL; 1/125
sec at f4.5; ISO 640.

Secured for another night

Even though the waters away from
Kulusuk's harbour are locked shut with
newly frozen ice, occasional 'leads' of
water allow locals to travel around the
island, potentially to hunt or fish. After an
excursion, this boat is secured to a stake
in the frozen-over harbour.

Canon 5D Mark II + 17-40mmL; 1/350
sec at f6.7; ISO 320.

Storm inbound

The view from Kulusuk towards Tasiilaq across the fjord looks forboding with yet another winter storm forecast. These two buildings are uninhabited - a common sight in smaller communities where many choose to move to larger villages in search of better prospects.

Canon 5D Mark II + 17-40mmL; 1/125 sec at f4; ISO 125.

Hunter with his rifle

Even the hardiest Greenlanders
occasionally need to wear head and hand
protection during the coldest months of
the year. For much of the time, however,
they wear far less protection than those
new to the Arctic. The small calibre rifle is
kept with its fur sleeve until it is required
to dispatch a seal or other sea mammal.

Canon 5D Mark II + 17-40mmL; 1/125
sec at f4; ISO 160.

Dawn breaks

The sun finally breaks over the coastal
mountains, bathing the landscape in a
warm glow. It is a welcome change from
the forbidding, cold blueness which
usually makes navigation difficult due to
low contrast.

Canon 5D Mark II + 17-40mmL; 1/125
sec at f19; ISO 100.

Dogs rest with vigilant hunters

Any slight ripple or movement on the broken, thin ice just 'offshore' might indicate a seal is close by. The Inuit hunters must stay attentive and react quickly with their rifle should the opportunity arise. The dogs are well used to the routine of hunting days and so take the chance for rest - kept warm by their thick fur.

Opposite
Canon 5D Mark II + 17-40mmL; 1/125 sec at f6.7; ISO 100.

Near
Canon 5D Mark II + 17-40mmL; 1/125 sec at f4; ISO 125.

Success but still not home and dry

After over five hours and shortly before
sunset, a seal is shot around a hundred
yards from the edge of the thick ice. The
body must now be recovered by paddling
the kayak across the skim of ice and
hooking it to the stern of the boat.

Canon 5D Mark II +17-40mmL; 1/125 sec
at f6.7; ISO 100.

Job done with clinical precision

Despite the seal having popped its head
briefly above the surface of the water to
breathe, it only took the hunter a split
second to quickly and humanely deliver
a killing shot to the head. It is a pragmatic
reality of life in the Arctic that sets the
sight of a dead animal against the pristine
beauty of the landscape. The seal will feed
the dog teams for many days.

Canon 5D Mark II + 17-40mmL; 1/125
sec at f4.5; ISO 100.

Time to turn for home

With the sun about to disappear once again, the two dog teams are quickly prepared for the considerable journey back to Kulusuk. Light levels deteriorate quickly and the temperatures plummet accordingly, so speed is key.

Canon 5D Mark II + 17-40mmL; 1/125 sec at f8; ISO 100.

Keeping eyes peeled

A local Kulusuk boatman, Lars, en route to
the Nagtivit Glacier to drop my team-mate
and me off for an expedition. We had
been followed by a minke whale and Lars
had always been one step ahead when
predicting where it would surface next to
breathe.

Canon 5D Mark II + 17-40mmL; 1/250
sec at f8; ISO 100.

THE DOGS

Investigating a new arrival

All working sledge dogs in Greenland
are kept outdoors year-round, exposed
to whatever conditions are thrown their
way. This is to maintain their robustness of
character. They are, however, very good
natured and inquisitive, especially with
new people. It's a different story with
other dogs or the local predators, polar
bears.

Canon 5D Mark II + 17-40mmL; 1/180
sec at f6.7; ISO 320.

Finding comfort in unlikely places

After the first six months or so, pups will lose their freedom to roam around their village. They will then, when not hauling sledges, be chained in groups around their owners' homes. This is to control breeding, prevent injuries from fights and to protect them from polar bear threats and fast moving skidoos.

Canon G10; 1/400 sec at f4.5; ISO 80.

Ski-mountaineering companions

Due to poor weather, my team and I
had a long, enforced stay in Tasiilaq
village, prior to an icecap speed record
attempt. Ski-mountaineering was the best
way to keep skills sharp and muscles
conditioned. We would always have
company in the shape of two local pups.
They would serve as excellent scouts,
finding routes through the complicated
and steep white-out shrouded mountains.

Canon G10; 1/2000 sec at f4; ISO 80.

Variety and lineage

Although dogs working in the Arctic are often referred to collectively as 'huskies', only a small number in fact are. The only dogs permitted in Greenland are the traditional Greenlandic sledge dogs which differ in appearance and temperament from Siberian huskies. Their coats vary from jet black to an off-white, with plenty of variety in between.

Canon 5D Mark II + 17-40mmL; 1/180 sec at f5.6; ISO 320.

One paw down

The dogs, once at their destination, in this case a hunting spot on the sea ice, are always still keen to run together and explore the area. To try and control their enthusiasm, a selection will have a front paw fed through their harness, encouraging them to settle down and wait for the next part of the journey.

Canon 5D Mark II + 17-40mmL; 1/125 sec at f11; ISO 100.

Time off from a life in the harness

Due to the excellent insulation provided
by their thick coat, the dogs are able
to rest and even sleep on the coldest
of surfaces. Despite their wolf-like
appearance they do, however, lack the
enhanced blood flow to the feet which
naturally adapts grey wolves to life in the
cold regions of the world.

Canon 5D Mark II + 17-40mmL; 1/125
sec at f5.6; ISO 100.

Age-old techniques still employed

Due to the lack of trees in Greenland, sledges were, until western settlers arrived, made from driftwood and whale bones. Today the same design principles survive and the sledges are enormously flexible to allow for the rough terrain they must cover for many years and thousands of miles. A 'stamp' brake is added to the rear to stop the sledge when dogs are reluctant to obey.

Canon 5D Mark II + 17-40mmL; 1/125 sec at f9.5; ISO 100.

Fan formation traces

Dogs are driven in front of sledges in most indigenous communities around the world and each will develop a harness and rope 'trace' or 'tugline' system to suit the terrain. Greenlanders usually create a wide 'fan' hitch in preference to the 'gangline' hitch in order to help travel over rough, treeless ice surfaces.

Canon 5D Mark II + 17-40mmL; 1/125 sec at f9.5; ISO 100.

Staying put

The wooden harpoon in the rear jams the sledge in place, just in case the dogs decide to set off whether their human cargo is present or not! This tool is also used to test the safety of thin sea ice, to break holes in newly formed ice and to create vibrations underneath which can encourage seals to move towards hunting zones.

Canon 5D Mark II + 17-40mmL; 1/125 sec at f6.7; ISO 100.

Lead dog with his team

Lead dogs are picked from amongst the others by their keenness to work and their intelligence. Often, in well-known areas, dogs will require next to no instruction and navigate effectively on their own. The other dogs are divided into swing, wheel and team dogs.

Canon 5D Mark II + 17-40mmL; 1/125 sec at f4; ISO 100.

THE JOURNEYS

The long road home

Having hauled for over seven hundred miles without resupply, my team-mate George makes headway on the return leg of our Long Haul journey. The polar high-pressure of summer had begun to make conditions more stable.

Canon 1D Mark II N + 19-35mm; 1/4000 sec at f4.5; ISO 100.

Base camp

The sun sets after a day of ski-mountaineering near the Hahn Glacier. As a training expedition, the team were testing different tent designs. On the left is a tunnel style and on the right, geodesic. The layout and stability of tunnel tents when wind direction is predictable made them the victors.

Canon D60 + 19-35mm; 1/250 sec at f6.7; ISO 200.

Steep ski approach

On a training expedition to the mountains near the Sermilik Fjord, a number of first ascents were made. On this occasion, we skied in a pair through the valleys and up the slopes until the climb itself began. We were able to ascend during the night, since the sun only just dips below the horizon in July.

Canon D60 + 19-35mm; 1/20 sec at f4; ISO 400.

Surreal Cold War relic

Hundreds of miles from the coasts of
Greenland, high up on the ice sheet, lies
the American DYE II early warning station.
Abandoned in the late 1980s, going inside
it is a huge step back in time and the
massive structure causes an enormous
snow drift behind it. Its purpose was to
give warning to the USA in the event of
Soviet missiles approaching from the east.

Canon 5D Mark II + 17-40mmL; 1/500
sec at f9.5; ISO 100.

Two hundred kilograms

In the early weeks of the 1374-mile Long Haul, our sledges weighed in at around two hundred kilos per piece. The effort taken to move these monsters took its toll. We would eventually lose around twenty kilos each in body weight.

Canon 1D Mark II N + 19-35mm; 1/2500 sec at f5.6; ISO 200.

The chill sets in

The sun can be remarkably warm in the Arctic, especially when you're working hard in the harness. Unless the 24 hour sunlight of mid-summer applies, the moment when the sun dips below the horizon beckons a cold night as the precious heat escapes up into the clear sky.

Canon D60 + 19-35mm; 1/90 sec at f6.7; ISO 100.

Job done

Following a successful first ascent of a coastal peak in mid-summer, my team-mate Rich makes his way down the ice slopes. The strong sun and reflection from the snow means that serious protection is needed to avoid burns.

Canon D60 + 19-35mm; 1/350 sec at f9.5; ISO 100.

A well protected home from home

As a storm cloud moves off to the east to reveal the sun, an expedition camp survives another night. Snow piled on top of 'valance' flaps and well placed anchors ensure that the aerodynamic tent can provide shelter in tough conditions.

Canon 5D Mark II + 17-40mmL; 1/125 sec at f9.5; ISO 100.

Climber prepares for crevasse

Adrian, a member of a film crew I worked
with in the winter of 2012, prepares
his ropework equipment. This glacier is
around twenty-five miles from Kulusuk.
Large crevasses were easily accessible and
proved ideal for filming interviews - with
both myself and Adrian filming suspended
on ropes.

Canon 5D Mark II + 17-40mm; 1/125 sec
at f4.5; ISO 160.

Optimum conditions

A day comes to an end on one of the few occasions when blue skies and light winds reign. The surface is hard with few sastrugi ridges and so progress can be made with relative ease. These opportunities would give rise to a 'make hay whilst the sun shines' policy and we would consequently ski longer days.

Canon 1D Mark II N + 19-35mm; 1/1250 sec at f5.6; ISO 100.

Navigating towards nothing

As part of my initial training expedition with my team on the icecap, I devised a triangular navigational route. On the inland ice, there are no landmarks for hundreds or even thousands of miles and so skill with compass and GPS is critical to future survival. There is no substitute for practice.

Canon D60 + 19-35mm; 1/90 sec at f6.7; ISO 100.

Irony

In the quest to travel across one of the
world's coldest wildernesses, it is bizarre
yet predictable that we met melt pools
and streams near the west coast at 74
degrees North. The long days accumulate
the sun's energy and the icecap forms
large melt systems whilst flowing towards
the coast or large 'moulin' sinkholes
which carve their way, often a mile down,
to the bedrock.

Canon 1D Mark II N + 19-35mm; 1/800
sec at f8; ISO 100.

Not an inch exposed

Despite the clear skies, wind and the
ambient cold can lead to injuries and
frostbite without proper precautions. Here
George wears a full face mask, goggles
and hood to protect his face from the
headwind. A slit in the mask allows his
breath to escape.

Canon 1D Mark II N + 19-35mm; 1/320
sec at f8; ISO 400.

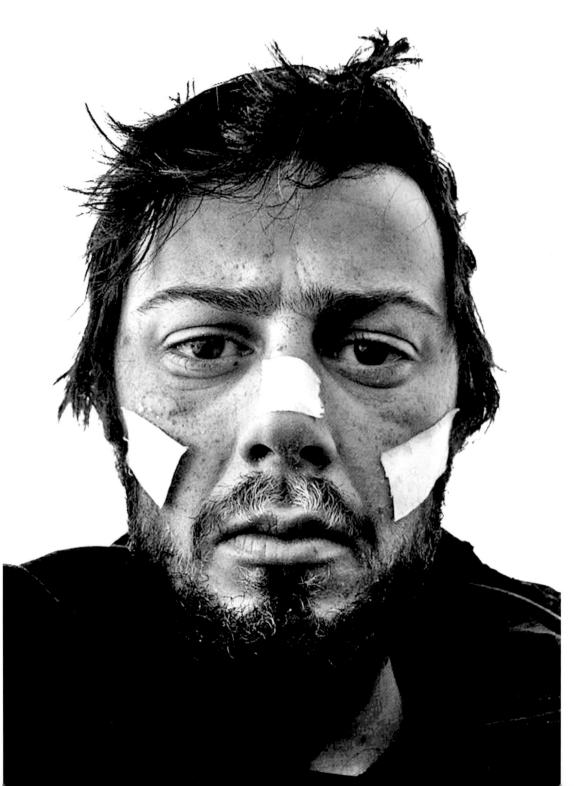

Brutal

The effects of 113 days unsupported on the Greenlandic ice sheet are apparent in these gritty images. We had both lost a quarter of our body weight.

Left: The Author, Right: George Bullard

THE ICE

An ominous weather front

Following a period of calm conditions for
sledging, a stark cloud front does not bode
well for the coming days. Within thirty
minutes the pair of us were enveloped in a
stubborn whiteout. It lasted for four days.

Canon 1D Mark II N + 19-35mm; 1/640
sec at f7.1; ISO 100.

True wilderness

The following photographs show the
many faces of the polar landscape and
ever-changing sky. The clouds would
often provide clues to future weather, as
well as providing much needed visual
stimulation.

Canon 1D Mark II N + 19-35mm; various
settings.

Not as flat as you would imagine

Icecaps, by virtue of the almost constant wind and regular snowfall, do not occur as a flat surface. They form sastrugi, hard ridges formed by drift, and elaborate patterns which mean that no two days or locations look the same.

Canon 1D Mark II N and 5D Mark II; various settings.

It is not all bad

There are occasions when the icecap
settles and behaves. The sun shines, wind
calms and the surface allows a sledge
to run smoothly. These days are the
reason why the handful of polar travellers
continue to ply their trade.

Canon 1D Mark II N + 19-35mm; 1/250
sec at f14; ISO 100.

Tortured ice

Common features of the hinge regions
which surround the icecap itself
are crevasse fields. These are most
pronounced in the late spring and
summer and are due to the ice flowing
and twisting downhill towards the sea.
Needless to say, with some being twenty
feet across and two hundred feet deep,
they provide a challenge to skiers.

Canon 5D Mark II + 17-40mmL; various
settings.

THE COAST

Near Isortoq

In a part of the world which is renowned
for its striking lack of colour in the cold
seasons, the summer is another matter. En
route to a filming project near the Hahn
Glacier, this view combines remaining
sea ice, rocky outcrops and a palette of
reflected colours.

Canon D60 + 19-35mm; 1/500 sec at
f5.6; ISO 100.

Icy remnants of the winter

Becoming ever smaller as melting and collisions break the ice apart, sea ice floats off Kulusuk in August (opposite) and a colossal iceberg as high as a cathedral moves along the coast near the Nagtivit Glacier. It may have broken off this glacier or from a number of others long the east coast.

Canon 5D Mark II + 17-40mmL; various settings.

A plethora of new opportunities

Due to the sheer inaccessibility and rugged nature of the Greenlandic coast, peaks which have not yet been ascended are plentiful. Many involve a challenging combination of mixed climbing over unstable rock and melting snow.

Canon D60 + 19-35mm; 1/350 sec at f9.5; ISO 100.

Sea fog on a perfect day

As a day to begin an expedition, it does not come much better than this. With clear blue skies and non-existent wind, my team-mate and I were delivered by boat through the fjords to our glacier start point. The low level early-morning fog, which sporadically made navigation a little more testing, lifted shortly after.

Canon 5D Mark II + 17-40mmL; 1/500 sec at f8; ISO 100.

Fishing near to home

Photographed from the edge of the
harbour area in Kulusuk village, local
fishermen cast lines in the bay to the north
of the island. Greenlanders have, in most
cases, abandoned the use of kayaks in
preference of glass fibre or aluminium
boats with outboard engines.

Canon D60 + 19-35mm; 1/1000 sec at
f5.6; ISO 100.

Floating chicanes

Depending on the origin of the ice, from
frozen sea water or calved from a glacier,
and the salinity of the sea water, ice floats
in varying ways. This is due to the relative
density and often the vast majority of
an iceberg can reside under the surface.
Some are the size of buildings and can
invert violently without warning.

Canon D60 + 19-35mm; 1/500 sec at f8;
ISO 100.

Simplicity

Even on monochromatic days such as
this, it is hard to not be enchanted by the
shapes, patterns and grandeur of the polar
and arctic environment. The iceberg in the
upper right corner is over a hundred feet
in height, not including its vast bulk below
the surface.

Canon D60 + 19-35mm; 1/250 sec at f8;
ISO 100.

Isolated outpost

The only source of warmth and shelter for some distance, this outbuilding near Kulusuk stands out against the stark polar night sky. Due to incessant snowfall and wind drift, a sole 'earth moving' truck works daily to clear routes to various parts of the settlement.

Canon 5D Mark II + 17-40mmL; 1/20 sec at f4; ISO 1600.

Icy grave

Photographed during filming for a
Greenland winter documentary, this hole
in the ice was created after a substantial
amount of ice axe work. The purpose was
to show the difference in reaction to cold
water when a person jumps in with and
without a waterproof immersion suit. I
was the unlucky subject.

Canon 5D Mark II + 17-40mmL; 1/60 sec
at f4.5; ISO 160.

Late dawn

The sun makes its first appearance in the depths of the Greenlandic winter. The cold associated with the dark hours makes the snow and ice safer. Only as the days lengthen into March and April will enough solar energy accumulate to begin the daily melt and longer term seasonal transition.

Canon 5D Mark II + 17-40mmL; 1/125 sec at f9.5; ISO 100.

Thick, thin and thinner...

On a crisp and cold January day, it is
possible to clearly see the various stages
of freezing that the sheltered waters
around the islands undergo. Strong first
year ice is on the left - thick enough to
stand a dog sled on. Ice only a couple
of inches thick comes next, thickening
as temperatures stay low, day after day.
Further out appears to be open water but
any attempt to cross it will find a thin skim
of ice. Strong winds can break this process
up in just a few hours.

Canon 5D Mark II + 17-40mmL; 1/125
sec at f4.5; ISO 100.

Inversion layer

One could be forgiven for thinking that this scene was photographed on a high altitude glacier with clouds far below. In fact, the team was only at 3000ft elevation and the phenomenon in the distance is an inversion layer over the sea. It is caused by an inverted temperature gradient where the air is coldest nearer to sea level.

Canon D60 + 19-35mm; 1/250 sec at f9.5; ISO 100.

Barren ice-locked coast

A flight along the coast of Greenland
in the early spring is one of the greatest
privileges a person can experience. The
awe never diminishes year on year. At
times it is possible to see bear tracks and
the ice behaves differently from day to
day, ensuring a new landscape every time.

Four photographs: Canon 5D Mark II +
24-85mm; various settings.